IMAGES OF WAR

8TH SS CAVALRY DIVISION FLORIAN GEYER

RARE PHOTOGRAPHS FROM WARTIME ARCHIVES

Ian Baxter

Pen & Sword
MILITARY

First published in Great Britain in 2023 by
PEN & SWORD MILITARY
an imprint of Pen & Sword Books Ltd
Yorkshire – Philadelphia

Copyright © Ian Baxter, 2023

ISBN 978-1-39906-281-7

Typeset by Concept, Huddersfield, West Yorkshire, HD4 5JL
Printed on paper from a sustainable source by CPI Group (UK) Ltd, Croydon CR0 4YY

Pen & Sword Books Limited incorporates the imprints of Atlas, Archaeology, Aviation, Discovery, Family History, Fiction, History, Maritime, Military, Military Classics, Politics, Select, Transport, True Crime, Air World, Frontline Publishing, Leo Cooper, Remember When, Seaforth Publishing, The Praetorian Press, Wharncliffe Local History, Wharncliffe Transport, Wharncliffe True Crime and White Owl.

For a complete list of Pen & Sword titles please contact
PEN & SWORD BOOKS LTD
47 Church Street, Barnsley, South Yorkshire, S70 2AS, England
E-mail: enquiries@pen-and-sword.co.uk
Website: www.pen-and-sword.co.uk
or
PEN & SWORD BOOKS
1950 Lawrence Rd, Havertown, PA 19083, USA
E-mail: uspen-and-sword@casematepublishers.com
Website: www.penandswordbooks.com

Freepost Plus RTKE-RGRJ-KTTX
Pen & Sword Books Ltd
47 Church Street
BARNSLEY
S70 2AS

✂ DISCOVER MORE ABOUT PEN & SWORD BOOKS

Pen & Sword Books have over 4000 books currently available, our imprints include: Aviation, Naval, Military, Archaeology, Transport, Frontline, Seaforth and the Battleground series, and we cover all periods of history on land, sea and air.

Can we stay in touch? From time to time we'd like to send you our latest catalogues, promotions and special offers by post. If you would prefer not to receive these, please tick this box. ☐

We also think you'd enjoy some of the latest products and offers by post from our trusted partners: companies operating in the clothing, collectables, food & wine, gardening, gadgets & entertainment, health & beauty, household goods, and home interiors categories. If you would like to receive these by post, please tick this box. ☐

We respect your privacy. We use personal information you provide us with to send you information about our products, maintain records and for marketing purposes. For more information explaining how we use your information please see our privacy policy at www.pen-and-sword.co.uk/privacy. You can opt out of our mailing list at any time via our website or by calling 01226 734222.

Mr/Mrs/Ms ....

Address...

Postcode................................... Email address...

Website: www.pen-and-sword.co.uk Email: enquiries@pen-and-sword.co.uk
Telephone: 01226 734555   Fax: 01226 734438
Stay in touch: facebook.com/penandswordbooks or follow us on Twitter @penswordbooks

Contents

About the Author

Ian Baxter is a military historian who specialises in German twentieth-century military history. He has written more than fifty books including *Poland – The Eighteen Day Victory March*, *Panzers In North Africa*, *The Ardennes Offensive*, *The Western Campaign*, *The 12th SS Panzer-Division Hitlerjugend*, *The Waffen-SS on the Western Front*, *The Waffen-SS on the Eastern Front*, *The Red Army at Stalingrad*, *Elite German Forces of World War II*, *Armoured Warfare*, *German Tanks of War*, *Blitzkrieg*, *Panzer-Divisions at War*, *Hitler's Panzers*, *German Armoured Vehicles of World War Two*, *Last Two Years of the Waffen-SS at War*, *German Soldier Uniforms and Insignia*, *German Guns of the Third Reich*, *Defeat to Retreat: The Last Years of the German Army At War 1943–45*, *Operation Bagration – the Destruction of Army Group Centre*, *German Guns of the Third Reich*, *Rommel and the Afrika Korps*, *U-Boat War*, and most recently *The Sixth Army and the Road to Stalingrad*. He has written over a hundred articles including 'Last days of Hitler', 'Wolf's Lair', 'The Story of the V1 and V2 Rocket Programme', 'Secret Aircraft of World War Two', 'Rommel at Tobruk', 'Hitler's War With his Generals', 'Secret British Plans to Assassinate Hitler', 'The SS at Arnhem', 'Hitlerjugend', 'Battle of Caen 1944', 'Gebirgsjäger at War', 'Panzer Crews', 'Hitlerjugend Guerrillas', 'Last Battles in the East', 'The Battle of Berlin', and many more. He has also reviewed numerous military studies for publication, supplied thousands of photographs and important documents to various publishers and film production companies worldwide, and lectures to various schools, colleges and universities throughout the United Kingdom and Southern Ireland.

Introduction

The 8th SS Cavalry Division Florian Geyer was formed in 1942 from a cadre of the SS Cavalry Brigade which was involved in operations behind the front line and was responsible for the killing of tens of thousands of the civilian population.

In the spring of 1943 it fought on the Eastern Front in the rear of Army Group Centre and took part in large-scale bandit actions with elements of various Wehrmacht and SS and police units. An estimated 3,000 Russians were killed, the great majority of whom were unarmed. The division was also responsible for poisoning all wells, and at least two dozen villages were razed in a scorched-earth policy to hinder the Red Army's advance.

The division was then moved to the Southern Front and took part in the German retreat to the River Dnieper. In October 1943 it was sent to Hungary where *Panzerjäger* and *Sturmgeschütz* armoured units were used as part of the division. It saw action and reorganization where it later operated in Croatia using new recruits drawn from Hungarians.

The division was trapped in the Siege of Budapest when the Soviet and Romanian forces surrounded the city in December 1944. The division was destroyed in the fighting for Budapest and, by the end of the siege, of the 30,000 men of the SS Corps, only about 800 reached the German line.

Chapter One

Birth of the
SS Cavalry Division

1939–42

The cavalry was an essential military element in the German army, despite its eagerness to become a fully motorized force. The Germans utilized horses both for draft and for riding into battle and they were a primary means of transport. While the infantry marched on foot, the supply chain was almost exclusively horse-drawn, carrying supplies and weapons behind rows of troops. Supporting the foot soldiers were cavalry brigades. A typical cavalry brigade had a strength of 4,200 horses for 6,200 men and comprised two regiments, an assorted regiment, an artillery battalion, a mechanized reconnaissance battalion and a bicycle battalion. Yet after 1939 most of the army cavalry was dissolved, apart from one division that was divided among mounted reconnaissance sections and convoy escorts.

Despite the reduction of the cavalry in the army, there was still a requirement for front-line cavalry troops and this included the new military arm of the SS. Although the SS were in their infancy by the time war broke out in September 1939, SS *Reichsführer* Heinrich Himmler wanted to build and expand his armed force comprising components of armour, infantry, mountain and cavalry.

From this idea the concept of the SS Cavalry Brigade was born under the command of Hermann Fegelein. It was based on the SS *Totenkopf* Horse Regiment raised in September 1939 for police and security duties during the invasion of Poland in 1939. Following the surrender of Poland in early October, the SS cavalry continued undertaking policing and security measures, enforcing laws, handling the deportation of Polish prisoners to work camps and rounding up and murdering anyone suspected of showing any type of resistance.

The SS cavalry were garrisoned in Warsaw and continued operating, mercilessly combating partisan activities as the war advanced elsewhere. As German hostilities with the West loomed and preparations were made by the Germans to attack the Low Countries and France, in April 1940 the SS Cavalry Brigade was expanded in size to comprise the 8th Sabre Squadron, 9th Replacement, 10th Heavy and

11th Technical Squadrons and a 12th Horse Battery of four guns. In May it was divided into two regiments: SS *Totenkopf* Horse Regiments 1 and 2, each of four squadrons; the 5th Heavy and 6th Horse Battery; and also included were Signals, Engineer and Motorcycle platoons. The SS cavalry performed well on the battlefield, but its successful operations were outshone by the blitzkrieg tactics of the Panzer divisions.

Following the Nazi victory in the West, in March 1941, as the German war machine prepared its might for an invasion of the Soviet Union, the SS cavalry brigade was renamed Cavalry Regiments 1 and 2. It consisted of the 1st, 2nd and 3rd Sabre Squadrons, 4th Machine-Gun, 5th Mortar and Infantry Gun, 6th Technical, 7th Bicycle and 8th Horse Battery squadrons.

Two days after the invasion of Russia, the 1st SS Cavalry Regiment was ordered to take part in a combat mission near Białystok. Soon after this operation, both SS cavalry regiments relocated from their garrisons in the East. Its commander, Hermann Fegelein, was determined that his SS Cavalry role in Russia would be aggressive and play an important part in destroying the Red Army. However, in reality the SS Cavalry and its Wehrmacht counterpart performed both offensive and defensive operations in pursuing Russian forces but were also engaging in limited combat. During the summer of 1941 the SS Cavalry Brigade comprising the 1st and 2nd Calvary regiments operated in the Pripet Marshes alongside the Wehrmacht's cavalry. By this time personnel were taken from the Sabre squadrons to form the brigade's Artillery, Engineer and Bicycle Reconnaissance squadrons. It was also given a light anti-aircraft battery. It now boasted a strength of 3,500 men, 2,900 horses and 375 vehicles. Here in the marshes the cavalry fought a number of hard-pressed battles. However, its cavalry did not just carry out military operations in the region; it also undertook a series of mass killings of Jews known as the Pinsk massacre. Over the course of a few days in early August some 8,000 Jews were killed. The murders were not isolated. Elsewhere the SS cavalry undertook a number of killings and at numerous times supported the widespread murders of Jews alongside the *Einsatzgruppen* (Special Action Groups or 'Death Squads').

Other murderous orders were issued to the cavalrymen as well: to 'pacify' the region, which included fighting against partisans, and to capture stragglers of the Red Army. The orders included killing enemy soldiers in civilian clothing, armed civilians and 'looters'. More than 15,000 Jews, partisans and soldiers of the Red Army were systematically murdered during September 1941.

From September onwards, the brigade continued its advance, operating alongside Wehrmacht units in Army Group Centre. In the region of Velikiye Luki and Rzhev they conducted a series of reconnaissance missions where they fought partisans. It was here that the brigade perpetrated further killings of 'suspected partisans' who were shot. The area was also heavily defended by Red Army units and the brigade saw some fierce fighting.

When winter finally set in, the Eastern Front stagnated and the brigade was forced to suspend operations and go over onto the defensive. Here the cavalrymen fought and defended until spring 1942. Losses had been significant and only half their brigade was combat-ready. More than 2,000 men had been killed, wounded or declared missing. A significant number of officers and non-commissioned officers had also been lost in action, considerably weakening the brigade.

In May the unit had no alternative other than to be withdrawn from the front and sent to Dębica in south-eastern Poland, where the SS had established a military training area. During its training and recuperation in the summer of 1942, it was decided that a new SS Cavalry division should be formed from the remnants of the SS Brigade, and the 8th SS Cavalry Division was born.

Herman Fegelein, a riding school owner's son from Bavaria who became a Nazi and eventually commanded a special riding school for the SS, which was established at Munich in 1937. Over the next couple of years former riding school trainees and instructors became the nucleus of the SS Cavalry. In Poland the SS Cavalry was for police and security duties. By the time the invasion of Russia was unleashed, two SS Cavalry Regiments had been formed and were used as auxiliary police units by the German occupation administration. (BA/Bender)

(**Opposite, above**) An early SS Cavalry brigade during operations in Poland in 1939. For war in Europe *SS-Reichsführer* Heinrich Himmler was determined to build and expand his armed force that was composed of armoured, infantry, mountain and cavalry divisions. *(BA/Bender)*

(**Opposite, below**) During the invasion of Russia an SS Cavalry Brigade can be seen here. Even from the beginning of the campaign on the Eastern Front the SS Cavalry Brigade had a dual function. The unit had both an ideological as well as a military function. If parts of the brigade were not fighting, the squadrons were required to police the rear areas in order to break any resistance in the region and to set up a military administration. The instructions often included killing enemy soldiers in civilian clothing, armed civilians and anyone seen in their eyes as hostile to the Reich. Jews were to be rounded up and executed, except for some required specialists such as craftsmen and doctors. *(BA/Bender)*

(**Above**) The first of two photographs taken in sequence showing cavalry soldiers washing and cooling down their animals in a river during operations on the Eastern Front during the summer of 1941.

The first of seven photographs taken on a parade ground showing recruits marching with their Karabiner 98k bolt-action rifle, which was the standard infantry rifle throughout the war. These men learned about combat, underwent a strict physical training programme and received political indoctrination. Perhaps the most important lesson that each one of them learned was that they were part of a closed order with its own rules and regulations. They soon learned the meaning of obedience, honesty and dedication to duty. *(NARA)*

Prior to parade practice soldiers can be seen here conversing, all wearing their SS M1938 field caps. Their M1935 steel helmets are neatly lined up on the parade ground with their stacked Karabiner 98k bolt-action rifles. *(NARA)*

A mortar crew shows off what they have learned in front of their trainers, commanding officers and other high-ranking soldiers. During training there were always hours of rigorous intensive schooling where the men had to learn about all aspects of their weapon, including learning from service manuals that contained detailed technical information and thorough instructions for handling the weapon. *(NARA)*

On the parade ground and the recruits can be seen waiting for their next instruction. *(NARA)*

An *SS-Obergruppenführer* can be seen here with his men on the parade ground marching around the perimeter. They are all armed with the 98k bolt-action rifle. *(NARA)*

Two photographs taken in sequence on the parade ground. It shows the recruits in file ready to take their stacked 98k bolt-action rifles while under the instruction of their troop commander. As in every army the soldier began with basic parade training which was interspersed with exercising, sports and endless marching. Strict guidelines were placed on the men for room and garrison order including uniform instructions and uniform treatment. Each week the training intensified and would include weapon training, first aid and specific arm of service training. The last phase of training consisted of group, platoon and company tactical training in which the soldier would learn how to behave on the battlefield and what their comrades expected of each other as a unit. *(NARA)*

Soldiers undertaking guard duties which were also a specific part of their training at the school. (NARA)

Two photographs showing cadets cleaning a number of Karabiner 98k bolt-action rifles in preparation for training and manoeuvres. The cadets would clean the weapon using the official designated rifle-cleaning kit known as the *Reinigungsgerät* 34, which was introduced in 1934. The kit consisted of a light steel can with hinged lid top and bottom, a chain pull-through, one large bore brush, an oiler and a cleaning tool or spoon for the receiver. (*NARA*)

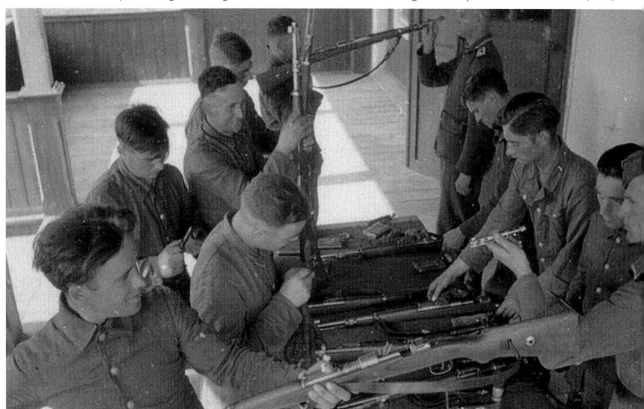

Cadets during a training exercise can be seen here marching and singing. Apart from military training, instruction at the schools was designed to communicate a sense of racial superiority and a connection to other dependable like-minded men, which included being ruthless and tough in accordance with the value system of the SS. Throughout their stay during training, cadets were constantly monitored for their ideological reliability and attitude towards their enemy. (NARA)

Recruits wearing the M1938 field cap. The soldier in the middle clearly displays the infamous skull-and-crossbones or *Totenkopf* insignia, both on his cap and collar. *(NARA)*

An *SS-Oberscharführer* points out a target to a young recruit during a training exercise. During their training development the cadets learned about small-arms techniques, physical training, hand-to-hand combat, orientation on the
ground, working with maps, digging and camouflaging, climbing training and overcoming water obstacles. *(NARA)*

Two photographs taken in sequence showing SS cavalry recruits singing. In both the Wehrmacht and especially the Waffen-SS, singing was an integral part of the soldiers' training. The songs they sang often represented a part of the soldier's life. It was about comradeship, of home and family, of a soldier's love and a soldier's death. Many of the songs they sang would eventually have the power to raise a whole company after a great action and enable them to renew their efforts to achieve victory. *(NARA)*

The first of six photographs taken in sequence showing recruits resting following a training exercise at the side of a lake with a rowing boat. A soldier can be seen playing an accordion in order to arouse camaraderie among the men. It was not only political, ideological indoctrination and military training that was part of the syllabus for all SS cadets, but being emotionally and mentally bound to each other was also very important. For this reason SS trainers often mixed training and pleasure as part of the curriculum. It was very important that there was a connection with other dependable like-minded men. (NARA)

Two photographs taken in sequence just prior to completing an exercise. The cadets can be seen here lined up ready for inspection. (NARA)

Cadets following an inspection are seen here conversing next to a lake. Note their Karabiner 98k rifles stacked upright together. This was common practice for riflemen if they needed to go quickly into action with their main weapon. (NARA)

Seven photographs taken in sequence showing cadets stripping down to their underwear and playing in the lake. While this allowed the men time to relax and build camaraderie, trainers looked upon this time as an opportunity to ensure that the men were at their physical peak. Throughout their training physical fitness was one of the most important aspects of the Waffen-SS regime and they ensured that various sports such as boxing, running, track and field, rowing and others were integrated throughout the day, thereby creating fit and healthy troops. (NARA)

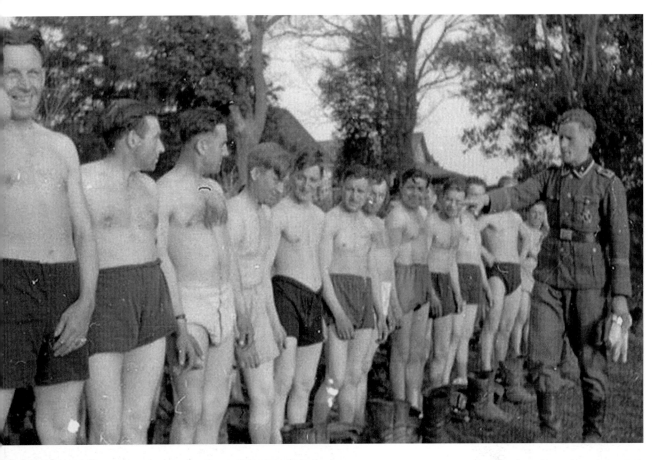

A pause during training in which three soldiers can be seen smoking. (NARA)

(**Above**) Just prior to a training exercise and soldiers are standing to attention while an *SS-Oberscharführer* reports to his commanding officer who can be seen giving the Nazi salute. *(NARA)*

(**Opposite, above**) An MG34 machine-gunner with his No. 2 are seen here leading a column of *Truppen* (troops) along a road during a training exercise. An *SS-Oberscharführer* accompanies the soldiers. *(NARA)*

(**Opposite, below**) The first of three photographs taken in sequence during a training exercise and showing an *SS-Oberscharführer* with the aid of a map conferring with one of his men, probably regarding their location and the route of their advance. The other soldiers can be seen sitting and listening. The other two images show the *SS-Oberscharführer* training his men with a Wehrmacht marching compass. This compass, manufactured by Busch D.R.G.M., had a black metal case made of nickel and brass, complete with signalling mirror and map scale measure. *(NARA)*

Two cavalrymen can be seen here conferring with the aid of a map. The motorcyclist is more than likely on a reconnaissance mission. Note the dismounted riders along the road with their horses. *(BA/Bender)*

A photograph taken inside a command post bunker on the Eastern Front. An *SS-Sturmführer* can be seen sitting at a desk surrounded by his men.

Chapter Two

Eastern Front

September 1942–December 1943

Following the creation of the 8th SS Cavalry Division, the unit was not immediately thrown into combat and was only deployed against the Red Army later because no other German formations were available in the Rzhev-Toropets sector of the front. Fighting in the Rzhev sector in the summer of 1942 was part of a series of battles that lasted some fifteen months in Army Group Centre. The 8th SS supported a number of Wehrmacht units from Model's 9th Army that were battling against stiff Russian resistance. Russian losses were high, but resistance was considerable and the 9th Army consequently managed to occupy the majority of the Rzhev salient. Although the SS Cavalry Brigade was outnumbered and outgunned, it still played an important role in encircling Red Army troops near Rzhev, for which its commander Hermann Fegelein was decorated. However, in spite of their successes, the SS Cavalry as a whole were not as well trained as units from the elite premier Waffen-SS divisions. Their infantry tactics often led to whole squadrons being wiped out. Only more experienced army formations that were often part of a larger offensive saw the SS Cavalry Brigade become more successful. Yet their spirit and determination in battle regularly brought about a number of victories. In a letter to *Reichsführer* Himmler, Hermann Fegelein described how a corporal of the 2nd Regiment who had received a head-shot in battle near Rzhev 'first reported being wounded, then his death', which the commander viewed as the ultimate proof of obedience. Yet, although there was great sacrifice and fortitude on the battlefield, the 8th SS were also involved in widespread killings of Russian PoWs.

Hundreds of enemy troops such as those at Turov saw the massacre of many prisoners. Fegelein's men also committed terrible war crimes by using captured Red Army soldiers as human shields at Basary. Fanaticism and incomparable brutality characterized the 8th SS on the battlefield. Although none of these units were classified as elite at this time, in the eyes of Himmler he was proud of them as they had a duty to destroy the enemy and could use whatever means they had at their disposal to do this, which also included murdering innocent men, women and children. Russia was a land ripe for plunder and he saw the 8th SS having a dual role on the Eastern Front. Throughout its operations during the second half of 1942 it was involved in both the destruction of the Soviet Jews and the fight against the Red Army. The cavalry brigade combined the characteristics of being part of a military arm and security police.

By this period of the war these mounted SS units had undergone not only a rapid but also a complex development. They had evolved into a killing machine with the men ideologically indoctrinated. The cavalrymen, like so many members of other German paramilitary units, had quickly adapted and become heavily embroiled in every step of the escalation of each radical racial policy that was ordered to them. The ranks were filled with young recruits and volunteers who had often been politically radicalized. Their radicalization helped them in Russia because many of the cavalrymen were not completely combat-ready. Instead they roamed the countryside as paramilitary units that could fill the 'security vacuum' in the vast newly-occupied territories behind the front. It was here that they could execute Himmler's orders of annihilation.

However, Himmler's need to perform police security duties in the rear areas frustrated Fegelein's efforts to continue fighting alongside the army in a military role. In the eyes of the *Reichsführer* he saw the 8th SS mainly as a police unit that was strongly motivated by National Socialism and a willing accomplice to the annihilation of Soviet Jewry. Thus by the latter part of 1942, the 8th SS had become exactly the instrument the *Reichsführer* intended it to be: an established force of ideological soldiers proficient in carrying out military tasks on a limited scale and cleansing an operational area of possible enemies including innocent civilians.

The majority of the cavalrymen obeyed their orders, however heinous they were. As a result they murdered the Soviet Jews and even perfected their own killing methods. Out on the battlefield their operational existence still continued and some units fought alongside the Wehrmacht in the Rzhev and Orel sectors in central Russia until the spring of 1943. Heavy fighting continued to engulf the front and the 9th Army planned the evacuation from the Rzhev salient in what was called Operation *BÜFFEL* (BUFFALO). The withdrawal from the area saw the SS Cavalry Division take part in a large-scale *Bandenkampfung* or 'bandit-fighting' operation. Bandits or *Banden* was the term chosen by German forces for special operations units used for combating bandits except in districts under military administration. The security warfare's aim was defined as 'complete extermination'. The directive called on the security forces to act with 'utter brutality'. The order saw the SS cavalrymen together with four Wehrmacht divisions and other SS and police units undertake 'cleansing of the enemy'. The result saw some 3,000 Russians killed, the great majority of whom had been captured and were unarmed.

The SS Cavalry performed their policing duties with terrible acts of violence. Their success in combating partisans and undertaking cleansing operations against the Jewish community saw one unit being used to assist in combating the Jewish ghetto uprising in April 1943.

In early April 1943 the liquidation of the Warsaw Ghetto had been ordered and plans drawn up by German authorities to remove the majority of the ghetto inhabitants and deport them directly to the death camps, notably Treblinka. Liquidation of the ghetto was undertaken on the eve of the Jewish Passover on 19 April. Its objective was to remove everyone within three days. However, the Jewish people, aware of their impending fate, were determined not to be removed without a fight. Most of the remaining 30,000 Jews had already gone into hiding and a number of areas of the ghetto had been turned into fortified positions. Although many of the streets were empty, they offered no escape route. Instead the Jews would resist until they were either killed or they surrendered.

On 19 April the Jewish ghetto erupted in a fierce battle with German units including an SS Cavalry Reserve Training Battalion from the 8th SS Cavalry Division. SS *Brigadeführer* Jürgen Stroop was put in charge to suppress the uprising. His past efficiency in dealing with unwanted populations in occupied territories had yielded great success. Now in Warsaw, his primary task was to brutally suppress the Warsaw Ghetto Uprising by increasing his men's firepower, destroying entire city blocks and conducting mass executions and mass deportations. His task force used for the operation comprised 821 Waffen-SS paramilitary soldiers from five SS *Panzergrenadier* reserve and training battalions and one SS Cavalry reserve and training battalion which consisted of some 400 men.

Over the days that followed Stroop's men fought a number of fierce battles with the resistance forces doggedly fighting from one fixed position to another. Although the defenders were poorly matched in terms of equipment and supply, a number of them were hurriedly positioned along the main streets. Across the ghetto Stroop's men continued combing the area for more hideouts using dogs and smoke bombs. Sometimes they flooded suspected hideouts or destroyed them with high explosives. For the next week until 16 May the last remaining insurgents carried on fighting until they were either captured or killed. During this period there was sporadic defence in a number of areas, but mainly it was Stroop's men patrolling the streets and smouldering houses looking for hideouts. The suppression of the uprising officially ended on 16 May, when the Great Synagogue of Warsaw was blown up. Some 13,000 Jews were killed in the ghetto during the uprising, half of which were probably burned alive or succumbed to smoke inhalation. Of the remaining 50,000 residents of the ghetto, almost all were captured and deported to the Majdanek and Treblinka death camps. The death toll report among the Germans varied, but it is considered that there were some 110 casualties, 16 of which were killed in action.

Once again the SS Cavalry had bloodied its hands against innocent men, women and children. The reserve battalion was then moved from Warsaw and transported to Russia where it supported the division's operations in and around Bobruisk carrying out further security measures until September 1943.

In September the division was moved to the Southern Front and took part in the German retreat to the River Dnieper. During this time German infantry and armoured units tried frantically to hold on to the receding front line. By October 1943, both the German Army Group Centre and South had been pushed back an average distance of 150 miles on a 650-mile front.

In order to strengthen the 8th SS Division it was pulled out of the front and rear areas in the Ukraine and sent to Hungary in October, where the *Panzerjäger* and *Sturmgeschütz* battalions were combined and the Reconnaissance Battalion became a Panzer Reconnaissance Battalion.

(**Below**) Two photographs taken in sequence showing soldiers standing in line listening to their commander's instructions prior to commencing operations in the field. They all wear the standard field grey uniform. Their equipment is that of a typical German infantryman consisting of the usual belt and cartridge pouches and the Karabiner 98k bolt-action rifle. (*NARA*)

(**Opposite, below**) Soldiers on patrol. Note the infantryman armed with a captured PPSh-41 Soviet submachine gun known as 'Shpagin's machine-pistol-41' (its designer was Georgy Shpagin). Russian soldiers would often equip platoons and sometimes entire companies with this weapon, giving them excellent short-range firepower. (*NARA*)

A night-time action photograph taken the moment a projectile from a well dug-in 8cm GrW 34 mortar was fired in anger. This weapon was the principal infantry mortar used by both the Wehrmacht and the Waffen-SS. Six were normally assigned to an infantry battalion's machine-gun company. (*NARA*)

Two soldiers are seen here removing an obstacle from their trench during operations on the Eastern Front. They are both near the entrance of their shelter. Many of these bunkers were known by the troops as small houses. (NARA)

A machine-gunner displaying a belt of bullets from the entrance of his bunker living quarters. (*NARA*)

A commanding officer observes dug-in positions along the front. In the Rzhev sector in Army Group Centre's zone of operations the 8th SS fought a number of battles that lasted almost fifteen months. Parts of the fighting were so intense that the front often stagnated, leaving both Wehrmacht and Waffen-SS units to build lines of fortified positions. (*NARA*)

Two photographs taken in sequence showing cavalry soldiers drinking from their mess tins. It was more than likely alcohol they were drinking, and highly probable that the beverage was vodka or a home-made vodka-based drink, which was quite commonly brewed by the Russians. (*NARA*)

A motorcyclist with his motorcycle
combination manhandles his machine
across a wooden railway bridge.
The soldier is more than likely on a
reconnaissance mission of the area.
Note the symbol painted on the front
of the sidecar indicating it was part of a
motorcycle platoon. (NARA)

A trench periscope can be seen here
overlooking a position concealed by
saplings. The periscope was an optical
device for conducting observations
from a concealed protected position.
The device was very effective, especially
during urbanized fighting where soldiers
often had to endure many hours or
even days in the same trench or
fortified position. (NARA)

The first of four photographs showing a well-concealed flak crew preparing their weapon for a fire mission against what appears to be a ground target. The first three images show tarpaulin sheeting covering much of the flak gun in order to protect it not only from dirt and dust particles but also to provide additional concealment. Although these light anti-aircraft guns were used extensively to deal with the regenerated threat of the Soviet Air Force, the recurring appearance of heavier enemy armour compelled many flak crews to divert their attention from the air and support their own infantry and armour on the ground in an anti-tank role. *(NARA)*

The first of two photographs taken in sequence showing mortar troops during an enemy action with their well dug-in 8cm sGrW 34 mortar. It was very common for infantry, especially during intensive long periods of action, to fire their mortar from either trenches or dug-in positions where the mortar crew could also be protected from enemy fire. *(NARA)*

(**Below**) Preparing for an enemy action, three photographs show the same heavy machine-gun troop with their 7.92cm MG34. A heavy machine-gun troop was provided with a tripod mount (Lafette 34) with a pair of leather carrying slings (Trageriemen), a long-range optical sight (Zieleinrichtung 34), at least two spare barrel carriers (Laufbehälter 34), a belt-filling device (Gurtfuller 34) and a number of 300-round metal cartridge cases, plus assorted cleaning equipment. (NARA)

(**Opposite, above**) During military operations in the summer of 1942 these infantrymen can be seen operating inside a burning Russian village. Note the soldier armed with the Karabiner 98k rifle with an attachable rifle grenade-launcher. This device was called the *Gewehrgranatengerät* or Schiessbecher (shooting cup). The 3cm Schiessbecher cup-type rifle grenade-launcher could be mounted on any Karabiner 98k and was intended to replace all previous rifle grenade-launcher models. The launcher could be used against infantry, fortifications and light armoured vehicles up to a range of 280m (306 yards). *(NARA)*

(**Opposite, below**) During early winter operations on the Eastern Front in 1943 and a soldier wearing the Waffen-SS winter reversible grey-side-out can be seen here surveying the destruction of an enemy position. The cavalry served a dual purpose, with some units operating in a military function combating Russian forces while others undertook security actions with total disregard for human life. The SS cavalrymen together with some Wehrmacht divisions and other SS and police units undertook a series of wide-sweeping 'cleansing operations of the enemy' with total brutality. *(NARA)*

(**Above**) The first of two photographs showing a machine-gunner and his No. 2 during a pause in the fighting. Both the MG34 and MG42 had tremendous staying power on the battlefield, and a well-deployed, well-supplied gun crew could easily hold a large area for some considerable time. *(NARA)*

MG34 light machine-gunners wearing the summer Waffen-SS camouflage smocks. In Germany the term 'light' defined the role and not the weight of the gun. The MG34 was extremely effective both in defensive and offensive roles against enemy infantry and troops. The Germans continuously deployed their machine guns in the most advantageous positions. (NARA)

An injured soldier is given a sip of water from a canteen by one of his comrades. During combat on the Eastern Front the 8th SS sustained high losses. This was attributed mainly to them being regarded as a second-rate SS division with their losses being replaced by ethnic recruits with little training. *(NARA)*

Part of a motorcycle platoon with their motorcycle combinations during a reconnaissance mission. The sidecars are armed with the mounted MG34 machine gun with drum magazine for local defence. *(NARA)*

Soldiers armed with the Karabiner 98k can be seen here embroiled in an enemy contact utilizing parts of a farmstead as defence against incoming fire. (NARA)

SS cavalrymen with their horses. These men were often ordered to perform the 'systematic combing of the rear areas' of the battlefield. The Cavalry Brigade was assigned to these duties because it was more mobile and better able to carry out large-scale operations. As a consequence it played a fundamental role in the transition from 'selective mass murder' to wholesale extermination of the Jewish population in many parts occupied by the Germans. (NARA)

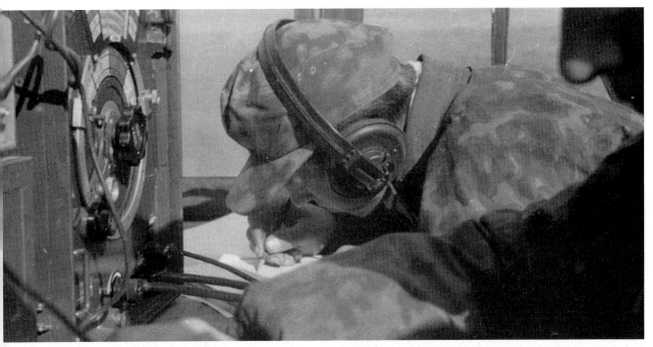

A soldier belonging to a signals battalion, which provided both field and radio communications support within the division, linking all subordinate units. Regiments and battalions had their own signals but only for internal communications. Telephone and radio troops were detached to all divisional units and laid telephone wires.

During the Warsaw Ghetto Uprising in April 1943 an SS Cavalry Reserve Training Battalion from the 8th SS Cavalry Division was used to help in the suppression. In this photograph SS troops walk past a block of burning houses during the uprising. (NARA)

SS troops guard members of the Jewish resistance captured during the suppression of the Warsaw Ghetto Uprising. (*NARA*)

An SS officer questions two Jewish resistance fighters during the defeat of the Warsaw Ghetto Uprising as *SS-Brigadeführer* Jürgen Stroop (rear, centre) and his security detail look on. (*NARA*)

Jews captured during the Warsaw Ghetto Uprising are led away from the burning ghetto by SS guards. Their fate was almost certainly to be transported directly to Treblinka and murdered. *(NARA)*

A pioneer unit with shovels. Their primary role was to assist other arms with tasks such as the construction of field fortifications, military camps, bridges and roads. *(NARA)*

A dismounted cavalryman on the outskirts of a village. During 'pacification actions' in the rear areas the cavalry would often without prior reconnaissance enter a village, riding at full speed, and ride out the other end, then occupy the outer edges of the village. In accordance with an agreed plan, it would then gather the whole population together, including women and children, for inspection. (NARA)

A Cavalry signalman with cable spool on the rear of the horse specifically for laying wire and cable for telephone connections. A signals battalion was charged with laying and maintaining the signal communications of the unit. The light motorized brigade, the cavalry brigade and each frontier guard sector had available one Signals Company. All of these signals units were fully motorized. (NARA)

Two of the troops in their foxholes wearing the Waffen-SS reversible anorak grey-side-out. The soldier in the forefront of the image is armed with the MP38/40 submachine pistol. *(NARA)*

Chapter Three

Croatia and Romania

December 1943–April 1944

When the division arrived in Hungary its units were reorganized in preparation for further operations. It now consisted of *Sturmgeschütz* and *Panzerjäger* battalions. The 8th *SS-Sturmgeschütz Abteilung* (assault gun) comprised the 1st Company with twelve StuG. III Ausf.Fs, the 2nd Company equipped with Pz.Kpfw.IV Ausf.Fs, the 3rd Company contained Pz.Kpfw.III Ausf.Js Mk IIIJ and StuG IIIs. Later the unit received a batch of StuG 42s. The 8th *SS-Panzerjäger (mot.) Abteilung* (tank-hunter) was equipped with three companies each of ten *Panzerjäger* 38, Marder Is or IIs and later the Hetzer (light tank destroyer).

The division comprised the 15th and 16th *SS-Kavallerie* Regiments, each consisting of two battalions of three squadrons. The 18th *SS-Kavallerie* Regiment had one battalion of three squadrons. Supporting the regiments was the 8th *SS-Artillerie* Regiment which was equipped with five batteries: the 1st Light Battery containing four 75mm howitzers; the 2nd Medium Battery with four 105mm howitzers; the 3rd Heavy Battery equipped with four 15cm howitzers; the 4th Self-Propelled Battery whose equipment was an unknown quantity of weapons; and the 5th Battery had six 21cm rocket-launchers (the *Nebelwerfer* 42). The 8th *SS-Flak Abteilung (mot.)* had three batteries of four flak guns (twelve 2cm) and three batteries of six flak guns (eighteen 8.8cm). It also comprised the 8th SS-Pioneer Battalion, 8th SS-Signals Battalion, 8th SS-Field Replacement Battalion along with supply and administration companies.

Because the division sustained huge losses on the Eastern Front, its units were replaced with many Danube Swabian recruits. These conscripts were a collective term for the ethnic German-speaking population that lived in various countries of south-eastern Europe, especially in the River Danube valley. Many of them were recruited in Hungary and Yugoslavia. In fact, Danube Swabians formed around 20 per cent of the population. Yugoslav Danube Swabians supplied more than 60,000 troops for both Wehrmacht and Waffen-SS military formations; some voluntarily but many more under duress. They all actively participated in the brutal repression of Yugoslav partisans and their suspected sympathizers, including 69,000 Jews living in Yugoslavia. It was here in Yugoslavia that the 8th SS was posted and undertook widespread anti-partisan operations in Croatia.

By this point in the war the partisans in Croatia had strengthened numerically and created more mobile combat units and gained control over larger territory. As a result the Germans deployed military units against the resistance groups, and in some areas managed to create large and successful attacks, pacifying some of the territory. The 8th SS, as it had done in Russia, carried out anti-partisan operations with fanatical ruthlessness, declaring whole areas populated with bandits, Jews, gypsies, spies or bandit sympathizers. During its short existence operating in Croatia it conducted hundreds of murders of Jews, bandits or suspects and villages were burned down. The soldiers were instructed that they were to indiscriminately shoot or preferably hang bandits, including women. Any sign of harbouring or sympathizing with the bandits and whole families were murdered. In the minds of many of the SS ideo- logically, since partisans represented an immediate threat, they were equated with Jews or people under their influence. As a result the systematic murder of anyone associated with them was an expression of the regime's anti-Semitism policy and was viewed by members of the Wehrmacht and Waffen-SS as a necessity of war. In the eyes of the SS, killing partisan 'enemies' was not just an immediate necessity, but was pre-emptive warfare against 'future' enemies.

By the spring of 1944 the division was pulled out of Croatia and returned to Hungary where it took part in the fighting in Transylvania after the front collapsed against overwhelming Russian attacks. By the end of March the division was renamed the 8th SS Cavalry Division Florian Geyer. Florian Geyer was a Franconian nobleman who had led the Black Company during the German Peasants' War between 1524 and 1525. Veterans from the division formed the core of the 22nd SS Volunteer Cavalry Division Maria Theresia following the latter's creation on 29 April 1944.

Already the Russian advance in the south had brought its armies perilously close to the borders of Hungary. Before panic had spread across the Southern Front, Hitler had ordered Operation MARGARETHE: the German occupation of Hungary. The operation was largely a Waffen-SS affair and consisted of second-rate SS combat formations being used as 'fire brigade' units.

Both the *SS-Panzergrenadier-Division Reichsführer-SS* and 18th *SS-Panzergrenadier-Division Horst Wessel* had taken up positions in Hungary by 16 April. Because Northern Transylvania was now under German military occupation, the 8th SS Cavalry Division moved its units into the area in order to defend the region against a Red Army advance into Hungary.

Between 8 April and 6 June, the Russians launched their offensive against Romania. A series of military engagements erupted, with the Red Army objective of cutting off vital Axis defensive lines in Northern Romania. However, both Wehrmacht and

Waffen-SS defensive positions were well dug in and the Red Army failed to overcome the German and Romanian defences in the region, but after regrouping and resupplying their forces in August the Russians then re-launched their offensive against Romania. The offensive began with a massive preparatory ground and aerial bombardment in order to soften up some of the strongest defensive positions. Some of these defensive lines comprised mazes of intricate blockhouses and trenches. Towns that fell in the path of these defensive belts were evacuated. Thousands of women, children and old men were removed from their dwellings and some were actually pressed into service to help construct massive anti-tank trenches and other obstacles.

Although it appeared that the Germans were prepared for a Soviet attack, much of the equipment employed along the defensive belts was too thinly spread. Many soldiers were unable to predict exactly where the strategic focal point of the Red Army attack would take place. To make matters worse, when the Red Army began heavily bombing German positions all along the frontier, it severely weakened the strongest defensive lines. From 19 August until the end of the month the Soviets launched a series of heavy ground and aerial attacks that were massive and relentless. During this period the Russians were able to break through the German defence lines. In order to avert complete destruction the 8th SS withdrew with high losses while the German 8th Army retreated to Hungary. Many German troops including some Waffen-SS units were cut off and captured. Those that were left fled towards Hungary as best they could, fighting the Romanians and Soviet forces which stormed through the Carpathian Mountains.

By early September Russian troops reached the Yugoslav frontier and on 8 September Bulgaria and Romania declared war on Germany. Two weeks later on 23 September, Soviet forces arrived on the Hungarian border and immediately raced through the country for the Danube, finally reaching the river to the south of Budapest.

It was here in Hungary where Hitler placed the utmost importance on defending what he called the last bastion of defence in the East. Against all military logic, he felt that it was Hungary and not the River Vistula in Poland that presented a natural barrier against an advance on Germany. For the defence of Hungary he was determined to use his premier Waffen-SS divisions, including *Totenkopf* and *Wiking* that were positioned along the Vistula. The 8th SS Cavalry Division, which had been driven out of Romania, was also going to support the premier divisions' attempt to halt the Russian advance.

In late 1943 the 8th SS was upgraded and received an assault gun company (*Sturmgeschütz Abteilung*). Six photographs taken in the winter show the 8th *SS-Sturmgeschütz Abteilung*. The *Abteilung* consisted of three companies of armour, but only the 1st and 3rd Companies had a complement of *Sturmgeschütz*. The 1st Company comprised twelve StuG. III Ausf.F variants, while the 2nd Company was equipped with Pz.Kpfw.IV Ausf.F variants and the 3rd Company contained Pz.Kpfw.III Ausf.J variants and StuG IIIs. Later the unit received a batch of StuG 42s. The 8th *SS-Panzerjäger (mot.) Abteilung* (tank hunter) was equipped with three companies each of ten *Panzerjäger* 38s, Marder Is or IIs and later the Hetzer. The StuG. III Ausf.F was armed with the 7.5cm StuK 40 L/43 long-barrel gun and the double-baffle muzzle brake. Throughout the mid-war years the assault gun provided crucial mobile fire support to the infantry, but despite its powerful 7.5cm gun barrel this assault gun was continually hard pressed on the battlefield and constantly called upon for offensive and defensive fire support, where it was gradually compelled to operate increasingly in an anti-tank role, something for which it was not designed. By 1944 tank-destroyers and assault guns outnumbered the tanks, which was confirmation of Germany's obligation to perform a defensive role against overwhelming opposition. (*NARA*)

A very muddy motorcyclist smiles for the camera and waves his arm in recognition to the photographer, who obviously finds the spectacle amusing. Many of the roads in Eastern Europe that the vehicles had to follow were often like a quagmire, frequently bringing a rapid drive to a crawl and hindering operations. *(NARA)*

Two photographs depicting a unit proudly showing off to commanding officers an Sd.Kfz.10 which mounts a PaK38 gun. Sometimes these vehicles had improvised armour, which meant the cab and engine compartment being armoured as well. This mobile anti-tank half-track was lethal in the field, but losses were high as the crew was quite vulnerable to enemy fire. (NARA)

Two photographs taken in sequence showing an *SS-Sturmführer* parading his unit in front of cavalry commanders next to an artillery tractor. *(NARA)*

Three photographs showing troops in various areas of operation during a security action, combing the countryside for partisan activity. Often the SS used the term 'anti-partisan operations' to conceal their ethnic cleansing and ideological warfare operations against perceived enemies such as Jews, or what they called Jewish Bolsheviks. Large-scale 'encirclement operations' were employed, which involved the use of the SS and supporting regular army units detached from the front line against the partisans. *(NARA)*

Commanding officers can be seen here walking along a dusty road during an anti-partisan operation. Due to the vast areas of terrain the SS had to cover during such operations, commanders often ordered their men to concentrate on short-term victories against the partisans. They regularly used military action against them, but invariably atrocities against civilians were carried out in order to try to pacify the regions. However, this resulted in a continuous flow of volunteers joining the partisan ranks. (NARA)

Two photographs showing a commanding officer with his men during a patrol. The anti-partisan operations instilled dread and fear into the population, but at the same time they also antagonized the locals, contributing to the growth and not the reduction of the partisan numbers. *(NARA)*

An *SS-Scharführer* can be seen here surveying the terrain through a pair of 6 × 30 Zeiss binoculars. The soldier next to him is armed with a Karabiner 98k bolt-action rifle. (*NARA*)

Soldiers moving quickly across a field during partisan operations. Their summer camouflage smocks blend well with the local terrain. (*NARA*)

Three photographs taken during a security action and soldiers can be seen conferring with the local peasants. While a number of towns and villages were not attacked by the SS, these operations repeatedly involved the annihilation of towns and villages regarded as potentially supporting the partisans, including burning buildings and murdering the inhabitants. The SS were also aware that informers in villages and towns could produce positive results and were sometimes friendly with the locals who would receive incentives and bribes for giving useful information. (*NARA*)

An MG34 machine-gun troop standing in a field. Two of the men, both ammunition-feeders, can be seen with their bullet belts around their neck. Note that the bullets point outwards in order to prevent the tips of the rounds digging into the men's necks. *(NARA)*

Soldiers are seen here queuing for rations from the back of a support truck during defensive operations in Romania. They all carry their mess tins. (NARA)

A soldier celebrating Easter in Romania can be seen here holding onto a goat and a basket of eggs.

Three soldiers can be seen here advancing through a field armed with the Karabiner 98k rifle. *(NARA)*

A commanding officer can be seen here using the Sf14Z scissor periscope. Although the periscope, commonly known as 'donkey ears', was able to estimate ranges, it provided only a narrow field of vision. *(NARA)*

Two photographs taken in sequence showing troops being decorated by their commanding officer during defensive actions in Romania in the spring of 1944. Between 8 April and 6 June, the Red Army launched the Jassy-Kishinev offensive. The operations consisted of a series of military engagements with the sole objective of cutting off vital Axis defensive lines in Northern Romania and driving German forces – notably the Waffen-SS – from their positions, including the 8th SS. (NARA)

A series of images showing a StuG.III Ausf.F from *SS-Sturmgeschütz-Batterie* 8 of the 8th SS. While drastic measures were made to ensure that infantry defended their lines, the assault gun forces were still being frantically increased to help counter the Russian onslaught. By this period of the war some 55 per cent of the German armoured arsenal consisted of assault guns that were now found in numerous units. The 8th SS used the StuG in a vital anti-tank role in order to desperately try to hold the Soviets back from breaking through their lines. *(NARA)*

Troops digging what appears to be a defensive position along the Hungarian-Romanian border. By the summer of 1944 the Russians had driven the Germans and Axis Forces across Romania into Hungary where the Waffen-SS were ordered to put up a defensive action in order to prevent the Red Army from advancing into the country. (NARA)

Inside a shelter along the front and a commanding officer surveys the terrain ahead through an Sf14Z scissor periscope. (NARA)

A 21cm *Nebelwerfer* 42 (21cm NbW 42) troop can be seen here with the HE (high-explosive) projectiles in their special transport frame crates. Note the crew setting up a tripod optic. This optic was similar to an artillery or anti-aircraft gun range-finder and would effectively and accurately estimate range to the target. This was critical to the success of a direct hit on the target. *(NARA)*

Out on a reconnaissance mission and a motorcycle combination can be seen passing along a road in a Hungarian village. Note the *SS-Oberscharführer* armed with the MP38/40 machine pistol sitting on the sidecar. The motorcycle is armed with the MG34 which can be seen mounted on the sidecar. *(NARA)*

Three young infantrymen clad in summer SS camouflage smocks share what appears to be sweets during a pause in operations. *(NARA)*

In a defensive position and an *SS-Untersturmführer* can be seen interrogating a captured Russian soldier with his men. (*NARA*)

Chapter Four

Hungary

November 1943–March 1945

In Hungary, the capital Budapest came under the direct command of General Otto Wöhler's Army Group South. Units committed to the defence of the Hungarian capital included the 22nd *SS-Freiwilligen-Kavallerie-Division* Maria Theresia, the 18th *SS-Freiwilligen-Panzergrenadier-Division* Horst Wessel and none other than remnants of the 8th SS Cavalry Division Florian Geyer, which was still licking its wounds from intensive fighting in Romania. These SS forces were not only employed to protect Budapest, but were also there to retain law and order and suppress any local uprisings. However, in October 1944 the Red Army had crossed the Hungarian frontier and was advancing towards the Danube in the direction of Budapest. The Soviet plan was to isolate Budapest from the rest of the German and Hungarian forces. After a temporary halt to recoup their men, the Russians resumed their attack in a massive wide-sweeping two-pronged advance that consequently saw the encirclement of the Hungarian capital and the entrapment of some 33,000 German and 37,000 Hungarian soldiers, as well as more than 800,000 civilians.

In desperation to hold Budapest and avoid the complete destruction of the troops trapped inside, Hitler wasted no time and ordered more troops to the area including his premier SS divisions.

On 26 December, the 6th Panzer Corps consisting of *Totenkopf* and *Wiking* were transferred from the Warsaw area and given orders to relieve Budapest. The attack was scheduled to begin in earnest on New Year's Day. Two attempts were made to relieve the city, but the 6th Panzer Corps was beaten back by strong Soviet forces. Consequently, for the next five weeks both *Totenkopf* and *Wiking* were forced onto the defensive and could only watch the beleaguered garrison struggle against large-scale Red Army attacks.

From late December until the end of January 1945 men from the 8th SS Cavalry put up a staunch defence. Fighting was so fierce that the remaining cavalry units were savagely mauled, but this did not prevent the troops from doggedly battling from one fixed position to another. Constantly the men were bombarded night and day by a hurricane of fire from Soviet heavy artillery. However, this did not deter the soldiers from resisting with fanatical determination to defend the city with every last drop of blood. Although the Germans were poorly matched in terms of equipment and supply, a number of the troops were hardened veterans that had survived some of the most costly battles in the East. Hurriedly these troops were positioned along the main roads leading into the city. Heavy machine-gun platoons dug in and held each end of the line while the remainder were scattered in various buildings. Armoured vehicles took up key positions in order to defend the main thoroughfare leading into the centre of the city, despite the fact that not one single tank was battle-ready. Crude obstacles were also erected and troops were emplaced in defensive positions armed with a motley assortment of anti-tank guns, flak guns, machine guns, *Panzerfaust* and the deadly *Panzerschreck*. For hours it seemed that each soldier was engaged in an individual battle of attrition. House-to-house fighting raged. Infiltrating the buildings, the Russians fought a series of deadly hand-to-hand battles with Germans using bayonets, knives and grenades. Anti-tank, machine-gun and mortar fire were brought to bear on anything that moved. German commanders were all too aware of the significant strength of their resilient foe and hoped that they could contain the Red Army for as long as possible until the premier Waffen-SS divisions relieved them from their hell. The Russians, however, continued mercilessly to tear through the suburbs of the city and lay to waste every building in their path. A mixture of armoured vehicles tried to save parts of the city from being overrun. The attack through the city was swift, but from every conceivable point German troops poured a lethal storm of fire onto the advancing troops.

By the end of January the whole city had been engulfed in a sea of smoke and flame. Slowly and methodically the Russians began taking one district after another, pushing back the defenders in a storm of fire and heavy infantry assaults. Whole areas were totally obliterated by tanks and artillery. Many Germans that were captured or wounded were executed on the spot and left suspended from the lamp posts as a warning to others. In parts of the city men from the 8th SS supported by a mixture of Wehrmacht and Panzer troops managed to knock out a number of Russian tanks with *Panzerfaust* and *Panzerschreck*, but even these courageous fighters were no match for hardened soldiers that had fought their way bitterly through Russia.

In order to save themselves from complete destruction, plans were made to evacuate the beleaguered soldiers trapped inside. On 11 February the remaining SS troops inside the burning city attempted to break out to the West. In the terrible battles that ensued, the fleeing SS troops of the 8th Florian Geyer and 22nd Maria Theresia were virtually annihilated. Out of the 30,000 SS troops that tried to escape, only some 700 of them eventually reached the 6th Panzer Corps lines. By 12 February Budapest was in Russian hands.

The remnants of the two decimated SS cavalry divisions were quickly absorbed to form the 37th *SS.Freiwilligen-Kavallerie-Division Lützow*. This newly-created SS division was strengthened by mostly underage German, Hungarian *Volksdeutsche* and ethnic Hungarian recruits. The division was intended to have three cavalry regiments of two battalions each, but due to lack of men and equipment it could only field two under-strength regiments as its main combat units. As a consequence it never reached the strength of a single regiment. Initially the division was commanded by *SS-Oberführer* Fegelein, but in March he was replaced by *SS-Standartenführer* Karl Gesele.

Almost immediately the new cavalry division was thrown onto the front lines fighting alongside the 6th SS Panzer Army in a new plan aimed at retaking Budapest. The plan, code-named SPRING AWAKENING, involved attacks by Wöhler's Army Group South, which would comprise the 6th SS Panzer Army, 8th Army, 6th Army and the Hungarian 3rd Army. The German and Hungarian force would attack south from the Margarethe defence lines, while the 2nd Army would attack from the west of the Russian lines. The planned pincer movement would crush the 3rd Ukrainian Front. As for the 6th SS Panzer Army, they would remain in the Margarethe positions around Lake Balaton. The Panzer army was commanded by *SS-Oberstgruppenführer* Sepp Dietrich and it consisted of the *Leibstandarte*, *Das Reich*, *Hohenstaufen* and *Hitlerjugend* divisions and the 37th SS *Freiwilligen-Kavallerie-Division Lützow*. Most of these divisions were newly arrived from the Ardennes offensive. However, they were not the same mighty SS combat formations that had previously fought in the East.

For the attack the *Leibstandarte* and *Hitlerjugend* were grouped together to form the *I.SS.Panzer-Corps*, while *Das Reich*, *Hohenstaufen* and *Freiwilligen-Kavallerie* formed the *II.SS.Panzer-Corps*. The operation was regarded as so secret that even the SS commanders were not allowed to reconnoitre the areas in which their units would operate in case the enemy began to suspect an operation was about to be mounted. All identifying SS insignia was also ordered to be removed and unit names were changed in a drastic effort to fool the Russians. However, when the SS undertook preliminary attacks, the Red Army finally detected a large body of Waffen-SS troops around the Lake Balaton area and quickly strengthened their defences by widening their mine belts and preparing anti-tank defences in depth. The Arctic conditions in the area also helped the Russians as it would make the SS advance more difficult.

During the early hours of the morning of 6 March 1945, Operation SPRING AWAKENING was finally unleashed. Although total secrecy about the attack had been lost, soldiers moving to the front were dropped off by their transport vehicles some 12 miles back from the launch-point of their attack and had to cover the remainder of the distance on foot. When they arrived many of the Waffen-SS grenadiers were soaked, freezing and totally exhausted. In fact, in a number of areas many grenadiers had not even reached their assigned jumping-off positions when the artillery barrage intended to soften up the Russian lines began at 0430 hours. Some commanders were so concerned about the state of their men arriving at the front that they asked for the attack to be postponed. However, these concerns were totally ignored. Instead, the grenadiers trudged out across the terrain through miserable conditions, reminiscent of fighting across the vast cold expanses of the Soviet Union. Because the area was marshy they were unable to be supported by armour and as a consequence were open to hostile fire. Although there were many losses in the Panzer Corps, these were elite SS grenadiers and their elan soon brought them across a succession of enemy trench lines where they went on to capture a number of tactically important areas of high ground. The *I.SS.Panzer-Corps* drove forward with great determination, driving the enemy back up to 25 miles in some places; however, they struggled against stiffer opposition and could only manage to penetrate the lines of some 5 miles.

Throughout the next few days of the operation the Waffen-SS battled its way slowly forward despite the losses and damage to their precious remaining vehicles. By 13 March it was clear to Army Group South that the offensive was failing and that the Red Army was preparing to go over to the offensive.

The Russian offensive, which Army Group South had forecast, finally opened on 16 March. Along the whole front the initial blows of the Red Army were so severe that they were able to bring Operation SPRING AWAKENING to an abrupt halt. Within hours of the artillery firestorm being unleashed onto the German positions, the 6th SS Panzer Army was in danger of being totally cut off. The divisions of the 6th SS tried desperately to fight on, but were being slowly battered into the ground. *Das Reich* doggedly held open a corridor of escape for its comrades, but the defection of the Hungarian army left the flanks wide open to the Russians. It was not long before Operation SPRING AWAKENING was routed, and for its troops to begin a full retreat or face total annihilation. By 25 March, the Red Army had smashed its way through the German defences and wrenched open a gap more than 60 miles wide.

Slowly but inexorably, the Germans withdrew. As for remnants of the 37th *SS.Freiwilligen-Kavallerie-Division Lützow*, its dishevelled and worn units limped across Hungary into Austria where they surrendered to American forces.

(**Opposite, above**) Seen here advancing along a road in Hungary is a *Jagdpanzer* 38t (Sd.Kfz.138/2), originally known as the *Leichter Panzerjäger* (38t) but later as the Hetzer. The 8th SS was equipped with the Hetzer in September 1944 and was incorporated into the 8th *SS-Panzerjäger (mot.) Abteilung* which was equipped with three companies, each of ten *Panzerjäger* 38ts, Marder Is or IIs and the Hetzer. These vehicles were used to equip tank-destroyer units of infantry divisions, *Panzergrenadier* divisions and independent units. They were often issued as replacements for lost battle tanks, a role for which they were not intended. They were equipped in all types of formations of the Wehrmacht and Waffen-SS in the last months of the war. Although the 8th *SS-Panzerjäger (mot.) Abteilung* was not supplied with many of these tank destroyers, it proved successful on the battlefield in Hungary.

(**Opposite, below**) A shelter on the front lines in Hungary. Along the German front a maze of intricate trenches was constructed in order to fortify positions during the Russian advance through Hungary. (*NARA*)

Two photographs showing a trench system along the front and two soldiers navigating their way through it. Parts of the defensive positions comprised crude obstacles where troops emplaced a variety of anti-tank guns, flak guns, machine guns, *Panzerfaust* and *Panzerschreck* in order to prevent the Russians reaching the Hungarian capital of Budapest. (*NARA*)

The first of three photographs taken in sequence showing an observation post. One of the soldiers wearing the animal-skin trench coat has what appears to be a wooden trench periscope. In the first photograph note the discarded PPSh-41 Soviet submachine gun. Sprawled out in front of the trench appears to be a dead Russian soldier, and it's probable that this soldier had been armed with the submachine gun. The last image (overleaf) shows one of the soldiers holding the PPSh-41. These captured submachine guns were used extensively by both the Wehrmacht and Waffen-SS during the conflict. *(NARA)*

The first of two photographs showing troops in a trench during defensive operations in Hungary. These trenches were constructed not only to defend the lines against advancing Russian forces, but also to keep the troops well-protected from the enemy's small-arms fire and substantially sheltered from artillery and tank salvoes. With the defenders sheltered, it often allowed them to kill approaching foes before they closed on a position. (NARA)

Inside a shelter and an infantryman can be seen checking his Karabiner 98k bolt-action rifle. *(NARA)*

A flak gun position in Hungary during defensive operations in early 1945. This weapon is clearly being used against a possible ground target. (*NARA*)

Two commanding officers can be seen here standing on a bridge, both wearing the reversible Waffen-SS anorak grey-side-out. Note the soldier on the left armed with the StG44 or *Sturmgewehr* 44 (Assault Rifle 44). This weapon was very effective, particularly during operations on the Eastern Front, offering a greatly increased volume of fire compared to standard infantry rifles. Many of the premier Waffen-SS divisions were the first to be issued with these weapons. (*NARA*)

A column of Sd.Kfz.251 half-tracks can be seen here advancing along a typical muddy road towards Budapest in March 1945. A stationary whitewashed Pz.Kpfw.IV is also shown.

A GrW34 mortar crew during a fire action inside a trench position. This weapon was the standard medium mortar in the Waffen-SS arsenal. It earned a reputation for being extremely reliable, accurate and having a decent rate of fire. A well-trained mortar crew often possessed the ability to engage in and out of action rapidly and with careful attention. They became renowned for their ability to quickly bring down fire on any adversary. The Germans used the mortar as an invaluable weapon and it was successful against hostile machine-gun emplacements, sniper posts or other enemy constructions in the front line that could not be effectively destroyed by rifle fire. (NARA)

(**Above**) A German-Hungarian command post outside Budapest in March 1945. The German officer can be seen conferring with his Hungarian ally with the aid of a map.

(**Opposite, above**) A column of armoured vehicles with winter-clad Waffen-SS soldiers from the 6th SS Panzer Army during Operation SPRING AWAKENING, the purpose of which was to retake Budapest from the Russians. The Panzer army consisted of the *Leibstandarte*, *Das Reich*, *Hohenstaufen* and *Hitlerjugend* divisions and the 37th *SS-Freiwilligen-Kavallerie-Division Lützow*, which consisted of the remnants of the 8th SS Cavalry Division.

(**Opposite, below**) A column of winter-clad Waffen-SS troops armed with a variety of weaponry including the MG42 marches along a road towards Budapest following a Tiger II of the sPz.Abt.509. In January forty-five of these Tigers were placed under the command of the 6th SS Panzer Army. By 9 February sPz.Abt.509 had only five operational vehicles remaining, with forty of them damaged and under repair.

(**Opposite, above**) An *SS-Unterscharführer* can be seen here crawling along the frozen ground among dead troops during operations in Hungary. The soldier appears to be armed with a Hungarian Femaru pistol. By mid-March 1945 the German positions in Hungary were smashed to pieces. In spite of heavy counterattacks and fierce unrelenting fighting, remnants of what was left of the 8th SS, now absorbed into units of the 37th *SS.Freiwilligen-Kavallerie-Division Lützow*, was in full retreat, escaping into Austria. Dishevelled, tired and worn out, the remaining units surrendered to American forces, ending their existence as an SS cavalry formation forever.

(**Opposite, below**) Armoured vehicles comprising half-tracks and *Sturmgeschütz* can be seen here halted on a muddy road near Lake Balaton during SPRING AWAKENING. These vehicles belonged to the 6th SS Panzer Army. The Sd.Kfz.251 on the left belonged to the *Leibstandarte*.

(**Above**) Waffen-SS troops around Lake Balaton. On 6 March 1945 the 6th SS Panzer Army spearheaded an attack against strong Red Army forces. On 16 March, the Soviets counterattacked in strength, and within hours the Germans were driven back to the positions they had held before Operation SPRING AWAKENING. A week later, totally outnumbered and with few armoured vehicles to repel the Russians, the 6th SS withdrew and took up positions elsewhere in Hungary. On 30 March, the Russian 3rd Ukrainian Front pushed back large German units defending Hungary and crossed into Austria. As for the remnants of the 8th SS Cavalry that had been absorbed into the 37th *SS.Freiwilligen-Kavallerie-Division Lützow*, they surrendered to American forces.

Structure of the SS Cavalry Brigade in Belorussia

July–August 1941

Brigade Commanders
SS-Standartenführer Hermann Fegelein (commander)
SS-Hauptsturmführer Karl Gesele (1st staff officer, deputy commander)
SS-Obersturmführer Anton Ameiser (aide-de-camp)

1st SS Cavalry Regiment
SS-Sturmbannführer Gustav Lombard (commander)
  1st Squadron: *SS-Hauptsturmführer* Waldemar Fegelein (commander)
  2nd Squadron: *SS-Hauptsturmführer* Ulrich Görtz (commander)
  3rd Squadron: *SS-Hauptsturmführer* Johann Schmid (commander)
  4th Squadron: *SS-Hauptsturmführer* Hermann Gadischke (commander)
  5th Squadron: *SS-Obersturmführer* Hermann Schneider (commander)

Bicycle Reconnaissance Battalion
SS-Sturmbannführer Albert Fassbender (commander)
  1st Squadron: *SS-Hauptsturmführer* Wilhelm Plänk (commander)
  2nd Squadron: *SS-Obersturmführer* Paul Koppenwallner (commander)
  3rd Squadron (anti-tank): *SS-Untersturmführer* Rudi Schweinberger (commander)

Supply and support units
  Engineer Squadron: *SS-Hauptsturmführer* Karl Fritsche (commander)
  Veterinary Squadron: *SS-Obersturmführer* Fritz Eichin (commander)
  Medical Unit: *SS-Hauptsturmführer* Otto Mittelberger (commander)
  Ambulance Platoon: *SS-Obersturmführer* Alfred Becker (commander)
  Light Cavalry Platoon (supply unit): *SS-Obersturmführer* Paul Hoppe (commander)

Brigade Artillery Unit
SS-Hauptsturmführer Arno Paul (commander)
  1st Battery: *SS-Hauptsturmführer* Arno Paul (commander)
  2nd Battery: *SS-Hauptsturmführer* Friedrich Meyer (commander)

2nd SS Cavalry Regiment
SS-Sturmbannführer Hermann Schleifenbaum (commander)
  1st Squadron: *SS-Hauptsturmführer* Stefan Charwat (commander)

2nd Squadron: *SS-Hauptsturmführer* Walter Dunsch (commander)
3rd Squadron: *SS-Hauptsturmführer* Hans-Viktor von Zastrow (commander)
4th Squadron: *SS-Hauptsturmführer* Kurt Wegener (commander)
5th Squadron: *SS-Hauptsturmführer* Herbert Schönfeldt (commander)

Winter 1941/42

Brigade commanders
SS-Standartenführer Hermann Fegelein (commander)
SS-Hauptsturmführer Karl Gesele (1st staff officer, deputy commander)
SS-Obersturmführer Anton Ameiser (aide-de-camp)

1st SS Cavalry Regiment
SS-Sturmbannführer Gustav Lombard (commander)
    1st Squadron: *SS-Hauptsturmführer* Waldemar Fegelein (commander)
    2nd Squadron: *SS-Hauptsturmführer* Ulrich Görtz (commander)
    3rd Squadron: *SS-Hauptsturmführer* Johann Schmid (commander)
    4th Squadron: *SS-Hauptsturmführer* Hermann Gadischke (commander)
    5th Squadron: *SS-Obersturmführer* Hermann Schneider (commander)

Bicycle Reconnaissance Battalion
SS-Sturmbannführer Albert Fassbender (commander)
    1st Squadron: *SS-Hauptsturmführer* Wilhelm Plänk (commander)
    2nd Squadron: *SS-Obersturmführer* Paul Koppenwallner (commander)
    3rd Squadron (anti-tank): *SS-Untersturmführer* Rudi Schweinberger (commander)

Brigade Artillery Unit
SS-Hauptsturmführer Arno Paul (commander)
    1st Battery: *SS-Hauptsturmführer* Arno Paul (commander)
    2nd Battery: *SS-Hauptsturmführer* Friedrich Meyer (commander)

2nd SS Cavalry Regiment
SS-Sturmbannführer Hermann Schleifenbaum (commander)
    1st Squadron: *SS-Hauptsturmführer* Stefan Charwat (commander)
    2nd Squadron: *SS-Hauptsturmführer* Walter Dunsch (commander)
    3rd Squadron: *SS-Hauptsturmführer* Hans-Viktor von Zastrow (commander)
    4th Squadron: *SS-Hauptsturmführer* Kurt Wegener (commander)
    5th Squadron: *SS-Hauptsturmführer* Herbert Schönfeldt (commander)

Supply and support units
    Engineer Squadron: *SS-Hauptsturmführer* Karl Fritsche (commander)
    Veterinary Squadron: *SS-Obersturmführer* Fritz Eichin (commander)
    Medical Unit: *SS-Hauptsturmführer* Otto Mittelberger (commander)
    Ambulance Platoon: *SS-Obersturmführer* Alfred Becker (commander)
    Light Cavalry Platoon (supply unit): *SS-Obersturmführer* Paul Hoppe (commander)

Order of Battle

Summer 1943

SS-Kavallerie-Regiment 1
SS-Kavallerie-Regiment 2
SS-Kavallerie-Regiment 3
SS-Artillerie-Regiment
SS-Radfahr-Abteilung
SS-Panzerjäger-Abteilung

SS-Flak-Abteilung
SS-Nachrichten-Abteilung
SS-Pionier-Bataillon
SS-Sturmgeschütz-Batterie
SS-Feldersatz-Bataillon

Autumn 1943

SS-Kavallerie-Regiment 15
SS-Kavallerie-Regiment 16
SS-Kavallerie-Regiment 17
SS-Kavallerie-Regiment 18
SS-Artillerie-Regiment 8
SS-Panzerjäger-Abteilung 8
SS-Aufklärungs-Abteilung 8
SS-Nachrichten-Abteilung 8
SS-Pionier-Bataillon 8
SS-Flak-Abteilung 8

SS-Feldersatz-Bataillon 8
SS-Sturmgeschütz-Abteilung 8
SS-Radfahr-Aufklärungs-Abteilung 8
SS-Ski-Battalion SS-Verwaltungsstruppen 8
SS-Sanitäts-Abteilung 8
SS-Veterinär-Kompanie 8
SS-Feldpostamt SS-Kriegsberichter-Zug (mot.) 8
SS-Feldgendarmerie-Trupp 8
SS-Krankenkraftwagenzug

Lineage

SS-Kavallerie-Brigade (August 1941–June 1942)
SS-Kavallerie-Division (June–October 1942)
8.SS-Kavallerie-Division (October 1942–March 1944)
8.SS-Kavallerie-Division Florian Geyer (March 1944–May 1945)

Commanders
SS-Brigadeführer Gustav Lombard (March–April 1942)
SS-Gruppenführer Hermann Fegelein (April–August 1942)
SS-Obergruppenführer Willi Bittrich (August 1942–15 February 1943)
SS-Brigadeführer Fritz Freitag (15 February–20 April 1943)
SS-Brigadeführer Gustav Lombard (20 April–14 May 1943)
SS-Gruppenführer Hermann Fegelein (14 May–13 September 1943)
SS-Gruppenführer Bruno Streckenbach (13 September 1943–22 January 1944)
SS-Gruppenführer Herman Fegelein (22 January 1943–1 January 1944)
SS-Gruppenführer Bruno Streckenbach (1 January–14 April 1944)
SS-Brigadeführer Gustav Lombard (14 April–1 July 1944)
SS-Brigadeführer Joachim Rumohr (1 July 1944–11 February 1945)

Chief of Staff
SS-Sturmbannführer E. von Elfenau (19 September 1942–8 April 1943)
SS-Sturmbannführer Hans Diergarten (8 April 1943–21 August 1944)
Oberstleutnant Sven von Mitzlaff (22 August 1944–45)

Area of Operations
Poland (March-September 1942)
Eastern Front, southern & central sectors (September 1942–December 1943)
Croatia, Czechoslovakia & Poland (December 1943–April 1944)
Hungary (April 1944–February 1945)

Manpower Strength
December 1942:   10,879
December 1943:   9,326
June 1944:   12,895
December 1944:   13,000

Appendix IV

Operation SPRING AWAKENING

Order of Battle: 6–15 March 1945

6th Army (Army Group Balck)

III Panzer Corps

1st Panzer Division
I./Pz.Rgt 24
Pz.Art.Rgt 73
3rd Panzer Division
Pz.Rgt 6
Pz.Art.Rgt 75
6th Panzer Division
S.Pz.Abt 509 (Tiger II)
Sturm.Pz.Abt. 219 (Brummbär)
356th Infantry Division

IV SS Panzer Corps

3rd SS Panzer Division Totenkopf
SS-Pz.Rgt 3
SS-Pz.Jg.Abt 3 (Pz.IV L/70(V))
Heers-Sturm. Art. Brig. 303
5th SS Panzer Division Wiking
SS-Pz.Rgt 5

6th SS Panzer Army

I SS Panzer Corps

1st SS Panzer Division Leibstandarte
   Adolf Hitler
SS-Pz.Rgt 1
SS-Pz.Jg.Abt 1 (Pz.IV L/70(V)
S.SS-Pz.Abt 501 (Tiger II)
12th SS Panzer Division Hitlerjugend
SS-Pz.Rgt 12 (Panther Ausf.G, Pz.IV
   Ausf.J, Flakpanzer IV 'Wirbelwind')
SS-Pz.Jg.Abt 12 (Pz.IV/L70)
S.H.Pz.Jg.Abt 560
37th SS.Freiwilligen-Kavallerie-Division
   'Lützow' (including *ad hoc* units of
   the 8th SS Kavallerie-Division
   Florian Geyer)
25th Hungarian Infantry Division
20th Royal Hungarian Sturm. Artillery

II SS Panzer Corps

2nd SS Panzer Division Das Reich
SS-Pz.Rgt 2 (Panther Ausf.G, Pz.IV
   Ausf.J, StuG. III)
9th SS Panzer Division Hohenstaufen
SS-Pz.Rgt 9
23rd Panzer Division

Pz.Rgt 23
Pz.Jg.Abt 128 (Pz.IV/70(V)

44th Volksgrenadier Division
Reichsgrenadier-Division Hoch und
Deutschmeister

I Cavalry Corps (mainly horses)
3rd Cavalry Division
Pz.Jg.Abt 69 (StuH 42)

4th Cavalry Division

2nd Panzer Army

LXVIII Corps
1st Gebirgs Division
13th Waffen-Gebirgs der SS Division
Handschar

16th SS Panzer Grenadier Division
Reichsführer-SS
71st Infantry Division

XXII Gebirgs Corps
2nd Hungarian Tank Division

118th Jäger Division

Luftflotte 4
II./JG 51 (Bf 109G)
II./JG 52 (Bf 109G)
I./JG 53 (Bf 109G, Bf 108)
I., III./SG 2 (Fw 190F, Ju 87G –
10.(Pz)/SG 2)
I., II, III./SG 10 (Fw 190F/G)
I./NSGr 5 (Go 145A, Ar 66D)

I./NSGr 10 (Ju 87D)
I./NAGr 14 (Bf 109G)
Stab/JG 76
JGr.101 – Royal Hungarian Air Force
(Bf 109G, Fi 156)
102 – Royal Hungarian Air Force
(Fw 190F)

Army Group E
(subordinate to Army Group F until 25 March 1945)

LXXXXI Corps
1st Cossack Division
11th Luftwaffe Field Division

104th Jäger Division
297th Infantry Division

Appendix V

Order of Battle

37th *SS.Freiwilligen-Kavallerie-Division Lützow*

Mainly consisting of underage German, Hungarian *Volksdeutsche*, ethnic Hungarian recruits and remnants of the 8th SS Cavalry Division:

SS-Kavallerie Regiment 92
SS-Kavallerie Regiment 93
SS-Kavallerie Regiment 94
SS-Artillerie-Abteilung 37 (two batteries
    with le.FH18 10.5cm)
SS-Aufklärungs-Abteilung 37
SS-Panzerjäger-Abteilung 37 (one
    company equipped with Hetzer)

SS-Pionier-Bataillon 37
SS-Nachrichten-Kompanie 37
SS-Sanitäts-Abteilung 37
SS-Nachschub-Truppen 37
Feldersatz-Bataillon 37

Appendix VI

Recruitment of the Waffen-SS

The following text is taken from the US War Department publication *Tactical and Technical Trends*, No. 35 (7 October 1943).

Recruitment of the Waffen-SS

Despite a general relaxation of requirements in the acceptance and induction of men for the German armed forces, rigid standards are reported to be maintained in the recruitment, within Germany, of that elite organization known as the Waffen-SS. Outside the German borders, however, standards are reported to have been lowered in the recruiting of *Volksdeutsche* (German-speaking persons domiciled outside Germany) and of non-Germans.

Because of this difference it is deemed advisable to consider Waffen-SS recruiting activities inside and outside Germany under separate headings:

a. Inside Germany

The basic conditions of recruitment are:

(1) A standard of physical fitness at least equal to that required by the Army.
(2) 'Aryan ancestry' and National-Socialist beliefs. Standards of height vary for different units. For the Adolf Hitler Bodyguard (*Leibstandarte*) the minimum is 5 feet, 10 inches. For the ordinary SS divisions it is 5 feet, 7 inches, or for men under 21 years of age, 5 feet, 6 inches. For mountain troops, the minimum is 5 feet, 5 3/4 inches.

Recruits are accepted in four categories, as follows:

(a) Volunteers for the duration
(b) Volunteers for 4½ years (with prospect of becoming non-commissioned officers)
(c) Volunteers for 12 years
(d) Officer candidates.

Age limits for volunteers for the duration are 17 to 45 years excepting that recruits for infantry, armored and signal units must not be more than 25 years old. Enlistment for the 4½-year period is restricted to men between 17 and 35 years of age and, for the 12-year period, to men between 17 and 23.

Officer candidates are classed either as 'technical' or 'active'. Age limits for the latter are 17 to 23 years. Preference is given to Hitler Youth leaders, Party functionaries and officials in organizations affiliated with the Party.

An 'active' officer candidate must serve a qualifying period of 12 months – six in a replacement training unit, six in a field unit – before going to one of the two SS officer training schools (*SS-Junkerschulen*). If he passes his preliminary tests there, he becomes an *SS-Junker*. When he is graduated, he becomes an *SS-Standartenober-junker* and is assigned to a unit. Promotion to *Untersturmführer* (2nd lieutenant) follows upon the recommendation of his commanding officer to the head of the SS.

Technical officers undergo much the same kind of training except that after six months of general military training they are attached for three months to the arm of service they have chosen, to learn the practical side, following which there is a three-month theoretical course.

While the Hitler Youth organization is the main source of recruits for the Waffen-SS it must be remembered that the Youth group is equally the main recruiting source for the Wehrmacht. As the HJ (Hitler Youth) has been actually as well as legally compulsory since 1940, the number of boys leaving that organization each year is now practically equivalent to a whole annual age class. Of these a small proportion, probably between fifteen per cent and twenty per cent are accepted as Party members and not all of these have in the past joined the Waffen-SS.

Since the beginning of 1943 strenuous efforts have been made to induce boys of 16 and 17 to join the Waffen-SS. Propaganda stories concerning SS troops in action frequently appear in HJ publications; SS men are detailed, together with representatives of the Wehrmacht, as instructors in the boys' military camps. There is reason to believe that in many cases the pressure exerted on the youths to 'volunteer' is tantamount to compulsory enlistment.

The Waffen-SS is not empowered to recruit from the Wehrmacht itself. Recruits already mustered for the Wehrmacht but not yet called up may volunteer for the Waffen-SS, but men who have been called to service or who are serving or who have served in the Wehrmacht are, as a class, placed outside the range of SS recruiting. Also, men with technical training or qualifications fitting them for service in the Air Force or in the Navy are barred from applying to join the Waffen-SS as officer candidates. There is one modification to these general prohibitions. Officers, and presumably enlisted men also, may be permitted to transfer from the Wehrmacht to the Waffen-SS in exceptional cases and at the discretion of the High Command. But there is no reason to believe that such transfers occur frequently or have any vital bearing on the recruiting problem of the Waffen-SS.

It is evident that the Waffen-SS is finding increasing difficulty in getting enough recruits by the voluntary method to replace heavy battle casualties as well as to maintain the present rate of expansion.

b. Outside Germany

Methods of recruiting have varied in the different countries, but a broad difference is discernible in the appeals made to the *Volksdeutsche*, to whom the German government can speak with a show of national authority even when they are citizens of another state, and the other nationalities who must be induced to enter the Waffen-SS on grounds of local or European patriotism.

The main groups of *Volksdeutsche* outside the Greater Reich are in Hungary, Rumania, Croatia and Slovakia. A report of January 1943 on the German minority in Hungary stated that 3,500 were serving in the Wehrmacht, 10,000 in the Hungarian militia and 20,000 in the Waffen-SS. Of the 70,000 *Volksdeutsche* from Rumania in the German fighting services, a majority are said to be in the Waffen-SS. In Croatia complete conscription has been introduced and all physically fit German males from 17 to 35 years of age, not already serving or otherwise exempt, are being called up for service in the Waffen-SS. Similar action has been taken in Slovakia. These are the first clear cases of wholesale conscription for the SS, though it can scarcely be doubted that there has been much pressure, if not actual compulsion, among the other *Volksdeutsche* groups. Several thousand *Volksdeutsche* from Russia have also been absorbed into the Waffen-SS.

The original decision to raise non-German forces to serve with the Waffen-SS was based on the propaganda rather than on the fighting value of the 'Germanic' volunteers. For this reason, apparently, the men were mostly organized in small national legions.

In Scandinavia and the occupied countries of the West, recruiting was done mostly by the local Nazi and Quisling parties; in the Baltic States it was done by the German-controlled governments; in the Balkans by German authorities in agreement with the governments concerned. In all these territories the Waffen-SS has obtained a virtual monopoly on recruiting for the German armed forces.

During the last six months, interesting changes have been noticed. With manpower becoming more important than propaganda, a larger element of compulsion has entered the recruiting campaigns, and at the same time the small, uneconomic legions are being reorganized into regiments and battalions, clearly intended to be incorporated into regular SS divisions.

In the occupied countries of Scandinavia and the West, the demand for recruits has been particularly noticeable since the early spring of 1943. The various Quisling leaders have addressed themselves especially to their followers, and demanded from them an offer of their services at the front as a test of their political integrity. The position has been most bluntly defined by the Senior SS and Police Leader, Rauter, in Holland. 'It is quite obvious,' he said in a speech in March 1943, 'that every SS man in his turn will have to experience battle on the East front. An SS man who thinks he cannot face this is not a true SS man and cannot become a leader. In principle, every SS man should apply for service at the front.'

In Estonia, Latvia and Lithuania the recruiting campaign is more intense. Considerable governmental influence has been exerted to make young men, members of the Civil Defense Corps and ex-soldiers join the Waffen-SS, or at least one of the auxiliary organizations of the Wehrmacht.

The head of the civil administration in Estonia recently told a gathering of Estonian SS legionaries that he was ordering all commissioned and non-commissioned officers of the former Estonian army, in conformity with their oath to defend the country, to join the SS legion, and that he was also contemplating the calling-up of younger age groups to bring the organization up to full strength. According to reports from various sources this was done and approximately 16,000 men were mobilized, the majority of whom seem destined either for the Estonian SS legion or for auxiliary service with the Wehrmacht.

The intensified drive for recruits in the occupied countries has been accompanied by a lowering of the physical and ideological standards demanded of them. The difference is best illustrated in Norway. In the original recruitment (1940–41) for *SS-Regiment Nordland*, men between 17 and 23, unmarried, Aryan and of good physique were invited to volunteer for one, two or four years. In 1941 the upper age limit was raised to 40 years. In the present recruiting campaign for *SS-Panzer-Grenadier-Regiment Norge* (replacing the *Legion Norwegen*), enlistment is open to all Norwegians between 17 and 45 years of age, whether married or single, with a minimum height of 5 feet, 5 inches.

In Latvia and Lithuania the recruiting notices ask for men between 17 and 45 years of age, Aryan, with no criminal records, and mentally and physically fit. This is probably now the general standard for the foreign SS recruits.

At the same time, less attention is being paid to the political and racial qualifications of recruits. Apart from the mass conscription of Croats and Estonians, there have been other indications that Nazi ideology is no longer regarded as an indispensable qualification. In Norway the advertisements for what are described as 'peaceful Waffen-SS duties' inside the country assure prospective recruits that enlistment carries with it no political ties. An even greater tolerance has been shown in the Balkans, where a Croatian SS division has been formed of Catholic and Moslem Croats. The acceptance by the Waffen-SS of recruits who are neither Germans, 'Aryans' nor Nazis and who are of a race and religion essentially alien to Europe suggests that the original conception of *SS-Tauglichkeit* ('Aryan' ancestry and National-Socialist beliefs) has been abandoned.

It is clear that recruiting of *Volksdeutsche* and non-German elements for the Waffen-SS is mainly determined by the political situation in the countries concerned. Where the population is considered reliable the SS are prepared to do mass recruiting; where it is unreliable, a measure of selection is still deemed necessary. Hence with *Volksdeutsche* and the Baltic populations, among whom a considerable degree of pro-German or anti-Russian feeling may be reasonably expected, an amount of pressure has been used which is hardly distinguishable from general conscription. In Scandinavia and the Low Countries, where the population is in general anti-German and the Quisling governments are not firmly established, recruiting is voluntary and appeals mainly to those who have already taken sides with Germany. Finally, the Croatian division is purely an opportunist measure, exploiting the existing political and racial divisions in Yugoslavia.

The outstanding feature, however, is the difference between the SS recruiting inside and outside Germany and the consequent differences in kind between the various SS Divisions. That the SS will endeavor to guard against this dangerous dilution by providing the impressed or mercenary troops with German officers is almost certain. But even this cannot alter the fact that a potential source of disintegration has been introduced into the elite corps of National Socialism.

Notes